Learn to turn a windfall of wealth into a lifetime of wealth.

Discover the strategies necessary to take sudden blasts of cash and make them last, while still enjoying yourself.

Here, you'll find direct and straightforward advice for safeguarding your money while still enjoying it as you cruise onward through life, a long wealthy life.

Windfall Wisdom:

Sudden Wealth, Forever Wealth from specific investment advice and psychological strategies

by Dr. Jim Kay

Copyright © 2020 Jenna Say Quoi, LLC

All rights reserved. No part of this publication may be reproduced, distributed, or transmitted in any form or by any means, including photocopying, recording, or other electronic or mechanical methods, without the prior written permission of the publisher, except in the case of brief quotations embodied in critical reviews and other noncommercial uses permitted by copyright law.

Dedication:
To Jenna, my lovely wife and my three children May, Noah, and Catera who all want straight answers to financial questions.

Discover other titles by Dr. Jim Kay:

Fast FIRE: Rules for personal finance to quickly become Financially Independent and Retire Early

Financial Wellness: Prepare for retirement and the unexpected. Become financially healthy and positively change your life.

Choices: A story of how personal finance transformed a boy's life with easy steps and inside secrets anyone can follow.

The advice and information in this book are from research and exchanges with individuals and experts in their field. No identification with actual persons (living or deceased) or products is intended or should be inferred. The stories, characters, and entities are fictional. This book gives a broad overview of finance. The author and publisher are not offering legal, accounting, psychological, or other professional advice. No representation or warranty of any kind is offered or should be used or construed as an offer or recommendation for any security. Investors should seek professional advice for their particular situation. No assumption of liability is made as to the accuracy or completeness of the material. Furthermore, the content may include inadvertent technical or factual inaccuracies. All advice is subject to individual situations and financial fitness for individuals or institutions. Liability of loss is the sole responsibility of the person using this guide. Invest at your own risk.

Content

Chapter 1 - Year one will make or break you

    Broke and dead

    Meet Rod

    Don't be Rod

    When you first get your windfall, splurge (within limits)

    Wait a year before spending any more of the money, and during that year make a financial plan

    Your team

    Pay off all of your debts

    Plan for emergencies

    Safeguard your money in CDARs

Chapter 2 - How your mentality influences your spending

    Your spending habits will predict how long this money will last

    How you grew up will influence how you spend your money

    Steve is too loud for his rich neighbors

Chapter 3 - Specific investments with tips, tricks, and inside secrets

    The magical money machine: passive income

    Mutual Fund Investments: the easiest form of passive income to set up

    Dollar-cost averaging

    Set your lifeboat to weather any storm: Always have basic living expenses covered

    Setting up a bond ladder

    Finding the same index funds the rich use

    Create another account to cover expenses related to FUN

    Dividend Achievers Index

    Dividend Aristocrats Index: Dividend Achievers on Steroids

    Let your money see the world

    Rebalance

    Enough money for a pleasurable, comfortable retirement

    Monthly Expenses, Passive Income Investment

    The key to a good retirement is not just money

- Dream Bigger Fund
- Jeff lives off $2 million a year

Chapter 4 - Hiring the right people
- Building your team
- Your financial advisor
- Advisor, when can I buy the toys?
- Insurance
- Your attorney
- Your accountant: fiscal superhero
- Your GateKeeper

Chapter 5 - Where to live
- When and where to buy a house
- Buying vs. renting a home

Chapter 6 - Psychology behind your windfall
- With this money, I'm feeling numbness, fear, with a touch of excitement
- I'm feeling unworthiness, resentment, guilt, with a touch of revulsion
- With this money, I've stopped enjoying life
- This money has brought stress
- I don't want to come across as being spoiled
- I don't want to come across as being selfish
- I inherited a company

Chapter 7 - Your money's impact
- Making promises
- A relative or friend has a business idea
- Leaving a legacy
- If you enjoyed or got something out of reading this book

Chapter 1 - Year one will make or break you

Broke and dead

The fact is SEVENTY percent of people with sudden wealth wind up bankrupt, and FIFTY percent of people who have a sudden loss of wealth end up dead not long after that loss. If you don't handle your sudden wealth the right way, at best, you'll end up broke, back where you started, or even worse broke and dead. If broke and dead doesn't sound appealing, then you'll want to embrace the following three simple steps along with the specific investment advice, psychological guidelines, tips, and tricks that follow in this book.

The three simple steps:
1. Spend 5% (and no more than 5%) right away on something frivolous and enjoyable, either a vacation or anything else that will *not continue to cost you money*. Translated, this means: Stay away from yachts and expensive cars. Or if you must, simply rent one for a week or two.
2. Put the rest of the money in safe investments for a year. I'll explain what we mean by "safe" in due course. During that year, consult with an hourly-paid financial advisor to develop a plan for long-term wealth management.
3. Set aside thirty times your basic living expenses into stable, "DO NOT TOUCH" investments that will cover your essential cost of living for the rest of your life. Plan for the worst to happen. You need enough money to fall back on and continue a decent living, even if everything else goes to hell in a handbasket. This book will tell you exactly where to invest your money. Finally, use the straight-forward, easy to understand tips and tricks, especially designed for the suddenly wealthy, found in this book.

Meet Rod

Rod is a guy who had every dream come true, only to come crashing down worse than where he started, but at least he was still alive.

Rod was a fifty-year-old bachelor who lived in a small town in suburban New York. He had an OK job that paid enough money for him to cover his monthly expenses on a one-bedroom apartment in a safe neighborhood. It also included a leased car, along with his food and clothing, and left a bit for entertainment; Yankees tickets, etc. He had no savings to speak of, as he spent all his income on his day-to-day living expenses. Even while living on this modest scale, he had racked up significant credit card debt.

But then, one glorious day, a registered letter arrived from California telling him his long-lost great-aunt Tillie had died at the ripe old age of 99, leaving him a sum that could have made him a man of independent means … if he managed it right. But Rod didn't handle the money well. He immediately quit his job. The yacht purchased cost thousands of dollars per year for maintenance and storage. He didn't pay off his credit cards; instead, he got more. He also bought a one-bedroom condo near the top of an elegant Manhattan residential tower with sweeping views of New York. The place was expensive and required monthly dues and costly maintenance.

With what remained, he lived comfortably for just under a year on the inheritance. When the money ran out, he ramped up his already significant credit card debt even more to support his lifestyle. He realized he was about to crash and burn as his credit cards maxed out.

Declined credit cards caused embarrassment at dinner. Rod could no longer afford either the yacht or the condo, both of which he sold at a loss. He moved back into a one-bedroom apartment, where the much smaller chunk of money he got from the sale of his yacht and condo lasted him for another year of relatively modest suburban living. Rod drove around a newly leased Camry looking for another job. He eventually succeeded in finding a job, and found himself right back where he started before receiving Aunt Tillie's gift, but this time with even more credit card debt.

Forethought, planning, and self-discipline could have given Rod a comfortable life for decades, not one glorious year and another relatively modest year.

Don't be Rod

Well, at least Rod remained alive and was able to pay his bills.

The people who end up broke after a windfall didn't create a financial plan to live off investments for years. They are people who did not recognize it as a *once-in-a-lifetime* opportunity to use time-tested, simple strategies to build lifetime security from the necessary foundation of a gifted nest-egg such as lottery winnings or the estate of great-aunt Tillie. The people who end up broke are people who do not follow the specific action-steps and psychological insights contained in this book.

You're one step ahead of the rest. You're already reading this book. You don't have to be another statistic, like the countless people who've blown through millions of dollars and wound up with nothing to show for it. This book covers the issues they've faced and the mistakes they've made and gives you advice on how to avoid the same bad habits that caused them to lose it all.

It's no crime to need some tutoring in financial tactics, strategies, and planning. Most people need guidance when it comes to managing their finances. This book is here to give it to you straight. If you've ever asked basic questions regarding investing, saving, and budgeting, you'll have ALL the answers you need to keep your money safe and let it grow.

This book pulls no punches. What you have here is a no-nonsense guide for serious people who want to get the facts fast, with no sugar-coating or glossing over difficult subjects. You want straight answers dished up succinctly. It also keeps it real, shoots from the hip, and tells it like it is. Nevertheless, you also want to have a bit of fun. That's why I'll start with the first order of business upon receiving your sudden wealth: enjoy a portion.

When you first get your windfall, splurge (within limits)

The money you now have is your windfall, your cash, your time to shine and have some fun. You've received a large chunk of money. Out of the blue, here it is. And you deserve to enjoy *part* of it right now. You deserve a taste of the high-life. But you also need limits. Call it *disciplined enjoyment*. Use a *maximum* of 5% of your windfall for immediate gratification and indulgence. 5% is enough for you to feel you spent a large enough part of it to have fun, but not too much that you think you wasted it. Have a blast, but not too much fun. Don't BUY anything that is going to cost you more money down the road. Don't buy a car that will cost more to insure or repair. Instead of a new watch that will cost money to service, repair, and insure, keep your old one. Instead of purchases that will continue to cost money to maintain, go on a family vacation. Use that 5% of your windfall to purchase leisure, make memories, and enhance relationships with family and friends.

It may seem cool to buy some object you've dreamt of owning for years. It might seem like a no-brainer to finally grab yourself that Ferrari 458 Spider you've always wanted, or many other luxurious bobbles and toys. And do you know what? It IS cool to indulge yourself with luxurious items and toys. But not now. The time will come when you can purchase your dream home or other expensive items. But cars lose value. So too do Rolex watches, and sometimes even real estate. So, what you want right now for your windfall is something else altogether.

Tip from someone who dealt with sudden wealth

Buying shit brought temporary happiness. Keeping up with that shit cost money and brought frustration.

Wait a year before spending any more of the money, and during that year make a financial plan

It takes time to develop a useful, robust financial plan. Those who do it quickly make mistakes. It takes research, due diligence, and careful study. It takes exploration, analysis, and scrutiny. More than anything else, this money will change how you think and what you want. If attacked in a rushed manner, none of these will be accomplished correctly and adequately.

This first year:
- Create a money plan with an hourly-paid financial advisor.
- Choose boring, predictable, non-exotic investments that offer a reasonable return with minimal risk and minimal expense. (Explained in full in the section: Safeguard your money in CDARs).

There are only three things you should spend money on at this early stage: the splurge mentioned previously, any taxes due on your windfall, and paying off *all* your debt (more on this topic very shortly).

Your team

Hire a team to help:
- Fee-based financial planner
- Lawyer
- Accountant
- GateKeeper (someone you can send money requests to)

The financial advisor you select should be a Certified Financial Planner (CFP) or a Registered Investment Advisor (RIA). This financial planner should be fee-based, charging you by the hour or a flat fee, rather than a financial planner who sells various financial products on a commission basis. If you don't go the hourly rate route or flat fee, the investment advice you receive may be biased. Your best interests may not be at the height of their plan, but rather it could be driven by the planner's scheme to maximize his or her commissions in servicing your account. You want a financial advisor who is working for *you,* and not as a sales rep for various financial investment firms.

Your financial advisor will create a plan that will include not just a well-thought-out investment strategy featuring a mix of stocks and other investments. It should also include a precisely defined monthly budget for your living expenses.

Pay off all of your debts

Debt is your enemy. Debt is a money-sucking beast. Debt takes and takes and takes. The money you owe is a greedy parasite, siphoning off precious dollars from your accounts in the form of interest payments. Debt is a monkey on your back. And we're not talking about a cute cartoon monkey hiding under a yellow hat. Get rid of the monkey. Pay off your debts.

At the same time, as you contemplate your splurge and before you spend the first 5%, pay off ALL your debt. Start with people you owe, then high-interest credit cards, then auto loans, then your mortgage. Do this all within the first week after you receive your windfall. *In short: if you have debt, pay it off.*

Gather all of your loan amounts together. If you have a manager who loaned you money to get by until your signing bonus was paid, pay the manager first. They probably also sent you a bill for a percent of your contract. Pay that off as well. If you owe friends or family money, pay them next. They lent you this money during your time of need; it's time to repay their generosity. Next are your traditional debts. Find the interest rate they are charging. Pay off the ones with the highest interest rate first and work your way to the lowest interest rate. If the money runs out as you're paying these debts, pay more than the minimum payment on the next debt with the highest interest rate.

As you're making those payments, examine the habits by which you accumulated that debt. Have you been living beyond your means? Did you fail to plan your finances before your windfall? Did you spend too much, too often on things you didn't need? Do you own unnecessary luxuries? Did you entertain too lavishly? Did you buy a new gas-guzzling Cadillac when a lightly-used, gas-efficient Subaru Forester could have done the job just as well? Did you buy a four-bedroom house when three or two bedrooms were all you needed?

Excluding extraordinary circumstances such as sudden medical bills, debt tends to result from overspending on things that *are not necessary*. If you're a person who has traditionally displayed little self-restraint, it will be way *too easy* for you to fall into the same pattern using this windfall. Show some restraint and wait to buy things that cost money to maintain. Buying crap without a plan will make your windfall shrink faster than a wool sweater in a hot dryer. Although it may seem ridiculous to have to control yourself with *all* this money, you need more restraint now than ever.

Make the decision now. Change your spending habits. Set yourself a budget. Make sure you can afford your purchases *and the cost to maintain those purchases*. A financial advisor will help you develop this plan. A simple and easily followed budget you could follow would be:

- 70% living expenses. Housing, utilities, food, fun, and insurance would all be paid from 70% of your monthly "salary."
- 20% big purchases. Trips, cars, jewelry, and furniture would be saved up and bought with 20% of your monthly budget. You might go a few months without buying a new toy because you are saving up for it. Once you have the money, buy it.
- 10% retirement. IRA, mutual funds, Roth accounts would be put aside every month for the future *you*.

Plan for emergencies

The Titanic only had enough lifeboats for one-third of the people. They didn't plan for catastrophe, but you will.

We live in an unpredictable world. Just like your windfall, so too can emergencies come out of the blue when you least expect them. Tornadoes hit, hurricanes make landfall, cars collide, jobs lost, health crises erupt, and a dozen different kinds of earthquakes (not just geological, but also mental, physical, financial, and emotional) can spring from nowhere at any time.

In anticipation of possible auto accidents, you strap into your seat belt when you get into your car. In anticipation of potential trouble at sea, you make sure your boat has enough life jackets for everyone on board, not to mention a reliable radio. Bear in mind that when the *Titanic* sank, more than a thousand deaths occurred purely due to a shortage of lifeboats. In your day-to-day life, you need another kind of boat – a financial lifeboat that can see you through and help you navigate any sudden sinking of your fortunes.

More precisely, you need eighteen months of living expenses set aside for emergencies. Most people need four months of living put away, but you're not most people. Your expenditures might vary widely given the life which will stem from your windfall. You might need to get your hands on a large chunk of cash quickly, and you won't want to have to sell investments to do it.

Where should you put this money? You have two choices, and they don't include hiding it under the cover of a lifeboat. You can put this money in a Money Market Savings Account. Alternatively, you can try to get a higher rate of return in a *target-date retirement account* with a target date ten years out. If you go the target-date retirement account route, you need to set aside not eighteen but rather twenty-four months of living expenses because this fund could drop in value. If it takes the same drop as the worst in target-date fund history, you'll still have a minimum of eighteen months of living expenses. Target date funds with a date ten years out are generally safer than target-date funds with longer timelines because they invest more in bonds and less in stock.

Safeguard your money in CDARs

Good for you. Right now, you are taking a year to work with a Certified Financial Planner and others to form a long-term approach to both preserving and enjoying your windfall in a smart, carefully mapped-out manner. Meanwhile, however, you need a safe place to park your funds, one where you can count on being paid a bit of income *without putting your capital at serious risk*. Minimize the risk of losing this capital, you have leftover after your splurge, taxes, paying off your debts, and setting up your emergency fund.

In this instance, you are dealing with a serious amount of cash, and the fact is that a simple Certificate of Deposit (CD), which only offers FDIC insurance up to $250,000, won't be adequate to handle it. What you'll want is a Certificate of Deposit Account Registry (CDAR), which is the best way to enjoy full FDIC insurance on multi-million-dollar accounts, while at the same time, receiving CD-equivalent interest rates. Start your search for these at cdars.com/. Put the money into accounts exclusively in your name with a beneficiary of your significant other or children. Money can change people. Access to this amount of money by other people may open them up to make bad decisions. They don't need the option to withdraw this money for their own reasons; reasons they may not even discuss with you ahead of time.

It's important to stagger the length of your CDARs so you could gain access to the money in three months, six months, and twelve months. Why? Well, if something comes up and you need a significant influx of cash (more than your emergency fund can handle) in three months, you will be able to get your hands on it without penalties. Without having any such emergency, when the three-month CDAR is cashed out, roll it back into another twelve-month CDAR. Note: An added benefit of CDARs is that they tie up your money in such a way you cannot readily get your hot little hands on it and misspend it. A CDAR is a handy tool for enforcing discipline on yourself.

Tip from someone who dealt with sudden wealth

Don't be in a rush to spend or invest your money. You'll be able to buy the cool shit and earn interest soon enough. For the first year, keep your money safe while you come up with a plan that makes sense to you.

Chapter 2 - How your mentality influences your spending

Your spending habits will predict how long this money will last

As the sayings go: Old habits are hard to break, or you can't teach an old dog new tricks. If you were a saver or a spender in the past, you're likely to continue this same approach. But now at higher dollar amounts.

If you've historically been a saver, you have no problem, except for perhaps being known among your friends and neighbors as a "cheapskate." But that's OK. Cheapskates usually come out on top when all is said and done. Stay on course, you penny-pincher!

But if you've historically been a big spender, you're going to have to mend your ways. Otherwise, the fact is, history has a way of repeating itself. If you overspent on entertainment, housing, cars, or clothing, you would continue to overspend in the same category unless you change your ways. Take the advice of Ba Jin, a Chinese novelist; "Only by not forgetting the past can we be the master of the future." If you were the type of person to spend everything you made, your windfall would be gone rather quickly unless you completely change your mindset and habits. If you lived paycheck to paycheck, up until now, you've had a poor person's mentality. If you don't change how you deal with and think about money, you'll end up wasting it and winding up back where you started. Don't go out and buy jewelry or cars worth more than your parent's house. Season tickets to Broadway won't make you look cultured. A giant fish tank in your living room won't bring about internal peace. You can't wear 400 pairs of shoes in any given year. Realize where you overspend and set limits.

The keyword here is *moderation*. If you were a spender and you want to continue spending, you can do so. *You just have to set (and ABIDE BY) limits*. You need a budget. You need to start caring about the YOU of the future. We all evolve. In the future, you'll have different wants, goals, and needs than you do today. Set aside money for that future *you*. After all, you're stuck with you for the rest of your life. You *can* change your mentality about money. And you must plan for the future. Invest in creating assets that will provide an income later. Your future self is worth it!

While you're planning to safeguard your future, consider what comfort level you want for your kids? Setting aside money for your heirs could ensure they and your grandkids benefit from your good fortune (See, Leaving a Legacy).

How you grew up will influence how you spend your money

The way you grew up relates directly to the lifestyle for which you are most comfortable. For example, if you grew up in the upper-middle class, you are used to eating in finer restaurants and driving newer, slightly more expensive cars. You feel most comfortable with this lifestyle and want to continue it. But if you grew up in the lower middle class, an older pickup truck and living in a smaller house will likely suit you just fine, no matter how much wealth you eventually possess. An excellent example of this is multi-billionaire Warren Buffet driving his pickup truck between his office and his modest house in Omaha.

One naturally feels most comfortable around people who were in a similar socio-economic level as they were when they grew up. That's why the once middle class, but now rich, most often want to continue to hang out with the type of friends they used to have before their windfall. The newly rich will down-play their wealth. They live in a comfortable but not ostentatious house and drive a car that is equally boring looking. They do this in the spirit of "not showing off," an attempt to keep their friends from thinking differently of them.

You shouldn't be ashamed of your sudden wealth. Simply make a point of knowing your lifestyle comfort level. Ultimately, you may get little pleasure from showing off your wealth. Don't change your lifestyle just because you now have the resources to do it.

Knowing your comfort level will help you realize:
- Happiness comes from being who you truly are
- You feel most comfortable around like-minded people
- You don't need to make rash decisions with this money, attempting to change who you want to be

Taking this first year to realize what's truly important to you is a good idea:
- Happiness comes from experiences and positive relationships, not things, toys, or items
- Once your basic living expenses are paid for by your income, happiness doesn't improve
- Income above your living expenses does improve how you feel about your accomplishments and how you feel about going to work

Steve is too loud for his rich neighbors

Steve found success in the music industry and moved to Las Vegas. He bought a house in an exclusive golf community right on the course. His view from his three-story home overlooks not only the golfers but the Vegas strip. Steve loves people and entertaining. Often, you'll hear people jumping from his third-floor balcony into the deep part of his pool. Golfers will be distracted by the skateboarders on Steve's half-pipe next to his pool, in view of the golf course.

Steve doesn't fit in. Neighbors think twice about inviting him to play bridge or meet for eighteen holes. Before you spend millions of dollars on a place to live, think about whether this money would be better spent on more land, where *you* can be *you*, where your friends can be as loud as you are—without people complaining. Where you can enjoy your hobbies without a knock on the door asking you to cut it out.

Steve didn't grow up poor, but he sure likes to have fun. People who did grow up in desperate economic straits and then became extremely wealthy are often sorely tempted to show off their newfound financial status. After years in a bug-infested, crap-ass apartment, they feel they are owed a mansion and all that goes with it. It's as if by demonstrating their new affluence, they can somehow wash away any perceived stigma of having "grown up on the wrong side of the tracks." It's as if they're saying: "Look at me. I'm never going back!"

In a way, showing off is understandable. After having gone so long "without," there is a natural tendency to want to become drunk in luxury, eat the best food, and drink the best drinks. After living like a piece of gum stuck to a shoe, there's a desire to take one's turn at commanding and being served; of enjoying your riches to the hilt.

But the same rules apply to the newly wealthy dirt poor and the newly affluent middle class: Excessive spending will leave you broke in the end, and right back where you started. And the YOU of the future will wind up cheated out of what you could have had.

Tip from someone who dealt with sudden wealth

I grew up dirt poor. Once I got paid all that money, I wanted to show the world I made it. I bought all the things that symbolize wealth. I had cars, jewelry, houses, boats. But with all that crap, I didn't have long-lasting happiness. I was who I was because of the trauma I dealt with in life. My teeth are now straight, but I still feel like that little kid from the block.

Chapter 3 - Specific investments with tips, tricks, and inside secrets

The magical money machine: passive income

Warren Buffett once said, "If you don't find a way to make money while you sleep, you will work until you die." Here, he's talking about passive income. It's not actually a magical money machine, but it sure does sound like one.

Imagine a magical money machine, called passive income, and it churns out genuine hundred-dollar bills regularly without you lifting a finger. You get unearned income for which you didn't have to do a lick of work. Sound good? Of course, it does!

Passive income is what you get when you own some form of capital:
- Bonds
- Stocks
- Dollars
- Natural resources (natural gas)
- Real estate (commercial or residential)
- Intellectual capital (copyrights, patents, and trademarks)

Passive income is the "rent" people or institutions pay for the use of your money, real estate, or the purchase of your natural gas.

Passive income is something the future YOU will want. Passive income is a golden ticket to Willy Wonka's glorious chocolate factory.

Mutual Fund Investments: the easiest form of passive income to set up

Mutual funds are one of the best long-term sources of passive investment income. Mutual funds invest in a variety of different stocks, sometimes referred to as a "basket" of stocks. Some of the top firms offering mutual funds include Fidelity, T. Rowe Price, Vanguard, Invesco, Northern Trust, and Schwab, each of which provides consumers with a broad assortment of mutual fund offerings. These range from funds that simply mimic the performance of the S&P or other indices to funds that specialize in specific industrial sectors such as transportation or digital technology. Each fund has professional fund management, trying to maximize your return.

When deciding which funds to purchase, look at the fees charged, and keep them low. A low fee is around 0.15%, usually charged for a mutual fund that simply tracks an index and therefore does not call for active management. Compare this to actively managed mutual funds, where fees may be as high as 0.8%. Compare the management fee for each mutual fund you're considering, but also compare the yearly rate of return as well. Make your decision based on these factors. When investing in mutual funds, buy with the idea you'll keep it there for the long-term, allowing it to grow. You'll learn more about specific mutual funds to look for in this section so that you can find the same index funds the wealthy use.

Dollar-cost averaging

Just like the stocks and bonds they contain, shares in mutual funds rise and fall daily in step with the market. It is virtually impossible to predict ahead of time when a fund's price will be relatively low, and when it will be relatively high.

To prevent buying at the wrong time, use "dollar-cost averaging." By investing the same amount of money in a given mutual fund each month over an extended period, you will naturally – almost organically – wind up beating the average cost. You automatically beat the average by buying fewer shares when the price is high and more shares when the price is low. A further benefit is that it insulates you from the prospect of investing all your money on a day when the price happens to be particularly high, only to see a price drop from which it takes time to recover.

Invest near the end of the month. Decide how many months or years, you want to pull money out of safe investments, and put it into the stock market. Divide the amount over that time and invest near the end of each month. The stock market typically sees lows near the end of the month and highs near the beginning of the month. Set automatic purchases to buy near the end of the month to take advantage of this little-known tip. The people who use dollar-cost averaging and buy near the end of the month, see a small but positive benefit to their rate of return.

Set your lifeboat to weather any storm: Always have basic living expenses covered

Let's call this lifeboat a "basic living fund."

Imagine you lose your job, your business ventures evaporate, you become extremely (and expensively) ill, and you simultaneously find yourself in court fighting (an expensive) civil case. Your life is upside down. Your ship is taking on water fast. You need your lifeboat.

That lifeboat, if you've planned correctly, will be thirty times your basic yearly living expenses. When crises strike, and all else fails, you'll always have this safe investment to continue frugal living.

To calculate the amount you need to squirrel away for your basic living fund, do the following:
- Figure the amount of money you and your family will need to get by on to purchase food, shelter, clothing, car, and other basic, *necessary* living expenses for one year. Do not include luxuries in your calculation. What you are coming up with is a bare-bones, no-frills budget. No trips to Tahiti. No hot tubs. No sporting event tickets.
- Multiply this figure by thirty to derive the amount you need to sock away.
- Put 50% of this sum into corporate bonds or preferred stock rated AA+ (Aa1 or Rank 2) or AAA (Rank 1) being even better. Use a bond ladder - described shortly.
- Put 35% into a Dividend Achievers Index mutual fund
- Put 10% into an S&P 500 Index mutual fund
- Put 5% into an International Index fund

This strategy spreads your investments across many sectors and gains the benefits of being in index funds. This investment mix avoids the risk of having a single fund manager who makes a mistake and invests too aggressively in one stock – and that stock proves to be a disaster, such as was the case with the ill-fated Enron.

With this approach, you can safely withdraw a fixed 3.5% each year. If you can live on $70,000 a year, you'll need $2 million in your basic living fund.

Setting up a bond ladder

Put your hourly-paid financial advisor to work. "Set up a bond ladder for me." Picture yourself climbing a ladder going up the side of a house. One hand clasps a rung, and the other hand grasps another level. One foot rests on a rung, and the other foot rests on yet another step. You have four points of contact with the ladder. Should an individual rung fail, you still have the safety of three points of contact. Staggering your bond investments takes away most of the risk of climbing that ladder (assuming you're sober).

Now imagine that each rung in the ladder is a specific company bond. In other words, each step represents a different number of years of bond commitment before maturity, along with a different company.

Half of your basic living fund is going to be in a bond ladder. To set it up:
- Decide how much you're willing to risk on each company, maybe $5,000 or $10,000
- Buy bonds in different companies over different periods, with maturity dates that overlap
- When one bond comes to maturity, invest the cash in another bond

This way, if one company were to fail and default on its bonds, you'd only be out what you were willing to risk in that particular firm's debt.

To further prevent loss, keep the bonds until they mature. Bonds you hold until maturity will have paid you the full interest over the life of the bond, as well – of course – all the money you paid as well. You get back the total dollar amount you paid and interest.

Beware of bond mutual funds. These funds have an increased risk of loss. During turbulent times, to service a large number of exits from the bond fund, the manager may be forced to sell bonds at a loss. Stock mutual funds, on the other hand, can be excellent investment vehicles.

Finding the same index funds the rich use

Maybe you can't get into the same clubs as the super-rich. Perhaps you can't get invited to the same parties or snag rides on their personal jets. But you sure as heck can enjoy the benefit of the identical investment vehicles as the super-rich, and there is nothing they can do to stop you!

Index stock mutual funds reduce risk by solely mimicking (rather than attempting to beat) the movement of key stock indices such as the S&P 500. These funds tend to have the additional advantage of low fees since they are not actively managed, but simply contain stocks which reflect the index. Some of the most successful investors recommend index funds for these reasons. All of the major nationally and internationally known investment companies offer index funds. Here are just a few of the most popular:

Fidelity
S&P 500
Fidelity 500 Index Fund - Investor Class (FXAIX)

MSCI EAFE International
Fidelity International Index Fund - Investor Class (FSPSX)

Vanguard
S&P 500
Vanguard 500 Index Fund Admiral Shares (VFIAX)

MSCI EAFE International
Vanguard Developed Markets Index Fund Admiral Shares (VTMGX)

Dividend Achievers
Vanguard Dividend Appreciation Index Fund Admiral Shares (VDADX)
Vanguard Dividend Appreciation ETF (VIG) Achievers

T. Rowe Price
S&P 500
T. Rowe Price Equity Index 500 Fund (PREIX)

Dividend fund, but not an index fund. Has higher fees
T. Rowe Price Dividend Growth (PRDGX)

MSCI EAFE International
T. Rowe Price International Equity Index Fund (PEIQX)

Schwab
MSCI EAFE International
Schwab International Equity ETF (SCHF)

Invesco
S&P 500
Invesco S&P 500 Index Fund (SPIAX)

Dividend Achievers
Invesco Dividend Achievers (PFM)

State Street Global Advisors
S&P 500
SPDR S&P 500 (SPY)

Dividend Aristocrats
SPDR S&P Dividend ETF (SDY)

MSCI EAFE International
SPDR MSCI EAFE Strategic Factors SM ETF (QEFA)

Create another account to cover expenses related to FUN

There's an adage: "If you're not having fun, it's your own fault!"

Yes, you've already splurged. You've enjoyed your trip to Paris or your chartered yacht cruise or your week at the Yankees Baseball Fantasy Camp. You've tasted the high-life and, at least for the moment, quenched your thirst for extravagant pleasure. But you'll want to have fun again sometime before you're 85. And why not? You're rich. Enjoy … *by spending money, you've carefully accumulated and allocated for that enjoyment.*

Picture yourself having a separate segment of your investments, the revenue (earnings) you'll dedicate to entertainment, vacations, tennis lessons, collecting autographs, amateur astronomy, or whatever.

Decide how much money you want to spend each year from your "fun fund." Multiply that by 25.

Allocate your fun fund money:
- 70% S&P 500 Index
- 20% Dividend Achievers or Aristocrats Index
- 10% in an MSCI EAFE International Index

The 70/20/10 mix reduces your risk of losing money in the stock market and gives you the best chance of financial success. You want to make money from these investments. This mix of 70/20/10 is the best approach to keeping fees low, diversification high, and following the trends of the stock market – worldwide.

S&P 500 Index

One of the most popular funds is the S&P 500 Index Fund. Investment companies create mutual funds that buy the same stocks this index follows. It's one of the most commonly followed equity indices on Wall Street. As Dow-Jones reports: "The S&P 500 is widely regarded as the best single gauge of large-cap U.S. equities … The index includes 500 leading companies and covers approximately 80% of available market capitalization." Many investment firms sell S&P 500 Index funds. Their primary purpose is to mimic the weighting and performance of the S&P. Such funds are not actively managed and therefore have relatively low management fees compared to actively managed funds. Such major Wall Street players as Warren Buffet often recommended S&P 500 Index funds to investors who want reliable returns balanced against a minimization of risk.

Dividend Achievers Index

Should you decide to be a bit more speculative in your investment approach, engaging with a slightly higher risk for the promise of slightly higher reward, you can do even better than the S&P 500. The Dividend Achievers Index has a high return rate average over the years, generally beating the S&P 500 of the same periods. One slight downside is that your money is invested in fewer companies, which means less diversification. But a compelling reason to use the Dividend Achievers Index is this: Companies that raise their dividends each year are proving they are growing and financially successful. The Dividend Achievers Index includes those companies that have increased their dividends each year for at least ten years. Here, you're looking at around 150 companies.

Dividend Aristocrats Index: Dividend Achievers on Steroids

If you REALLY want to beat the S&P, then you'll need The Dividend Aristocrats Index. This index has the fewest number of companies, but the companies, like 3M, Coca-Cola, and Colgate-Palmolive, are some of the best and most reliable in the nation. The Dividend Aristocrats Index includes those companies that have increased their dividends for twenty-five years *or more*. These companies have been around for a while, are "household names," and have continued success through decades. This fund is the least diversified, with only about fifty-five companies, but is less volatile (going up and down) compared to the S&P 500.

Let your money see the world

There's a heck of a lot of profit made overseas. Put the remaining 10% of your investment into an MSCI EAFE International Stock Index. Investing internationally avoids duplicating stock purchases in the United States and protects you from a drop in the value of the US dollar. This investment will give you broad diversification with around nine hundred different companies in twenty-one developed markets through Europe, Australasia, and the Far East while avoiding North America (already covered by the previous 90% you've invested).

Rebalance

Each year, in May, withdraw 4% for your fun. Why May? In most years, May typically sees high points in the stock market, and October sees a low point (more precisely, a beginning of a lull in the market). At the same time you make your withdrawal, also rebalance your fun funds back to a 70/20/10 split. If, after five years, you have more money in your accounts than you started, increase your withdraw to 5%. If you have less money, reduce the withdrawal percent.

Enough money for a pleasurable, comfortable retirement

You want a retirement in which you don't have to work (if you don't want to) while your money works aggressively to provide you with all the comforts you desire. If you have your emergency fund, basic living fund, and fun fund at the recommended goal amounts, you have enough to retire.

To make certain you can retire comfortably, do some basic math. In the year you retire, you need to have invested twenty-five times the amount of money you spend each year. Alternatively, you need *a stream of income equal to the amount of money you spend*. If you fully funded your basic living and fun accounts, you can safely withdraw 4% plus inflation each year. To give an example: When you retire, you can live on $20,000 a month, you'll need $7.2 million in investments. If you have costly tastes and need $100,000 a month, you'll need $36 million invested in your basic living fund and fun fund. To save you from having to wear out your calculator, here are some basic benchmarks using this formula:

Monthly Expenses, Passive Income Investment

$10,000	$3,600,000
$20,000	$7,200,000
$30,000	$10,800,000
$40,000	$14,400,000
$50,000	$18,000,000

You can do the math yourself. Figure the amount you need in passive investments so you could draw from your nest egg annually:

Monthly expenses
Multiplied by 1.2 (to pay the taxes)
Multiply by 12 months
Divide the total by .04

Or in other words:
(Monthly expenses x 1.2 x 12) / 0.04

The key to a good retirement is not just money

There are two things you need to keep in mind regarding your retirement:
- You must make sure you have enough money to keep you comfortable while you enjoy your retirement.
- You need to have *a plan for what you will do during your retirement*: activities to occupy yourself.

Even in retirement, you need to be active, energetic, and productive. A healthy mind stays engaged with the world. The people who live the most fulfilling lives in retirement are still learning, using their brains. Stay active with the community. Find a niece or nephew—get involved with their school. Focus your attention on a grandchild; get involved with their care. Volunteer your time, contributing to a worthy cause about which you have a passion. You don't have to work a traditional job, but you can if you'd like—anything to get you out the door and into the world. Old age is a state of mind.

Being lazy is the wrong choice. Those who aren't productive and feel engaged in society tend to become sick, both mentally and physically. A vacation is one thing, but a vacation from living isn't for you, or anyone. Retired people who don't take up a hobby or stay active in the community tend not to last long. If you think you can spend the time lazing about on a beach drinking your life away, rethink your plan.

Dream Bigger Fund

If your windfall is genuinely, really, actually big, consider a third investment: your dream big; dream bigger fund.

The dream bigger fund is is for *very* wealthy people. Perhaps you qualify. You already have your emergency fund, basic living fund, and your fun fund set up and good to go. The dream bigger fund is there to make genuinely huge dreams come true. Grant scholarships, build youth centers and buy mega-large ticket items with your dream bigger fund.

Your dream bigger fund will be a variable withdrawal investment. You decide how much as a minimum you'll have in your dream bigger fund. If the fund gets over your minimum, pull the extra out and enjoy it. If the value drops below your minimum, well … your dreams won't come true that year.

On the dream bigger fund, go after an investment that you feel will make you some serious, reliable money. Some possible choices include a business with a stream of income, rental properties, or aggressive growth mutual funds. If you would prefer the thrill of stock trading and have a bunch of money to invest, go with the Dogs of the Dow.

Buying the Dogs:
- On the last trading day of the year, in December, find the ten stocks on the Dow Jones Industrial Average that paid the highest dividends
- Invest equal amounts of money in each
- Keep the stocks for just over a year

You're buying those companies in hopes they'll do well again the following year. Typically they come out winners and have a high rate of return.

A less expensive way to invest is with the Flying Five. Also called:
- The Small Dogs of the Dow
- Puppies of the Dow

Invest equal money in the five Dogs of the Dow with the lowest share prices. People typically can buy shares in these companies more easily because of their lower share price. Therefore, they usually see higher returns.

Your dream bigger fund is for those who seem to have it all; those who could retire today or any time.

Jeff lives off $2 million a year

Jeff is a lot smarter than Rod. His fortune began with a simple suggestion from his dad. Jeff was a baseball player and, in his early 20s, went to the majors. He got an unusually large signing bonus and a contract that would make anyone happy. His father insisted he go to a financial advisor.

The first thing Jeff's advisor did was remind Jeff that only one out of five rookies last more than one year in the majors. Therefore, it was vitally important that Jeff safeguard most of his newfound wealth, placing it in safe investments that he and his then-girlfriend, and soon-to-be-wife could live off for the rest of their lives.

The hourly paid RIA (Registered Investment Advisor) told Jeff he needed $25 million in a mix of safe investments. Jeff was blown away, "I thought my signing bonus was huge, but I don't have that much!" Therefore, they put a large chunk into a "basic living fund," a mix of investments the couple could fall back on if necessary. The advisor took Jeff's monthly salary from the baseball team and gave Jeff some for his living expenses and invested the rest into the basic living fund. Jeff, an economical guy, lived off a third of the money the advisor put into his checking account. At the end of the year, the advisor split the extra money into two. A part went to fund the basic living fund further. The other half was used to begin Jeff's fun fund, a small, but a growing pot of money Jeff could use to travel and pay for large purchases.

Jeff had better luck on the field and in his career than most rookies. The advisor and Jeff got back together after the baseball player's contract was renewed. They continued to use the income from his salary to invest in Jeff's basic living fund as well as his fun fund. It would take two additional years to reach the $25 million goal in the basic living fund. If the career continued and a baseball salary kept coming in, Jeff and his fiancée could just sit back and watch it grow. If the career ended, they could withdraw money from it to live.

Jeff worked out the numbers with his advisor to get a few cool things. He paid in full for three cars and a boat. After their wedding, the couple rented a massive house in a gated community near other athletes. They lived very well on a monthly deposit to his checking account from his monthly salary. The advisor continued to invest the remainder.

Jeff's career lasted over a decade. Jeff, his wife, and kids kept their basic living fund. After it reached $25 million within the first three years, it continued to grow on its own without them having to add any additional money from his salary. When Jeff retired, the fund consisted of a bit less than $50 million. He and his wife pulled 3.5% from their basic living fund annually and continued to use the fun fund for trips and cool stuff for their kids.

Jeff's basic living fund:
- 50% individual corporate bonds rated AA - bond ladder
- 50% divided three ways
    - 70% Dividend Achievers Index
    - 20% S&P 500 Index
    - 10% MSCI EAFE International Index

Jeff puts the majority of his basic living fund, stock investment into the Dividend Achievers Index, because it is less likely to have as much of a loss compared to the S&P 500 fund.

Jeff's fun fund:
- 70% S&P 500 Index
- 20% Dividend Achievers Index
- 10% in an MSCI EAFE International Index

Tip from someone who dealt with sudden wealth

I set up a fund that could pay for all my necessary living expenses. Thank God I did. I've fucked up three times and had to live off that fund. Luckily, I came back, made some right decisions, and made it on top again.

Chapter 4 - Hiring the right people

Building your team

Jeff's success as a ballplayer wasn't based on his athletic talent alone. He was part of a team that, working together, excelled. The baseball team enjoyed an enormous amount of success against the competition on the ballfield. As was the case on the playing field, Jeff needed a talented team on his side to make his money grow rather than evaporate.

Like Jeff, you also need a talented team consisting of a financial advisor, lawyer, accountant, and GateKeeper.

This team will:
- **Financial advisor**
    - Put you on a budget
    - Guide you into a financial strategy based upon your wants and needs
    - Help you decide what luxuries you can afford to buy
    - Put your money into investments based upon your acceptable risk tolerance
- **Lawyer**
    - Protect you from lawsuits
    - Set up your Last Will and Testament
    - Set up trusts to protect your money
- **Accountant**
    - Reduce your tax liabilities
    - Makes sure you're paying taxes on time to reduce penalties
- **GateKeeper**
    - Stop people from bothering you for loans and handouts
    - Prevents YOU from looking like the bad guy who tells people NO to money requests

You need a team to make this money last for your future self. The most important person on this list is a financial advisor.

Your financial advisor

The investment plan laid out in this book will work well for people with a net worth in the millions. In your case, you might have a lot of money and need further direction.

You need a financial advisor to:
- Run the numbers and put you on a salary
- Set up your bond ladder
- Help you set up a basic living fund
- Help you set up your fun fund
- Give you the assurance you're investing into the right funds
- Help you decide how much and what type of insurance you need

Take your splurge trip, pay off your debts, set up your emergency fund, and then hire an hourly-paid financial advisor.

Take three things to your first meeting with your financial advisor:
- Specific goals, written down
- The investment plan you believe will work well for you (bring your emergency fund, basic living fund, and fun fund plans with you)
- A written description of the type of insurance you have with costs, deductibles, and coverage

The most important thing a financial advisor can do for a sudden wealth recipient is put you on a salary. You need someone who can tell you exactly how much money you can spend every month / every year, for this money to last a lifetime.

Therefore, the financial advisor will put you on a budget. Those who haven't fully funded their emergency fund, basic living fund, or fun fund will need to continue to invest a portion of their salary into these funds. Put 10% into retirement funds (basic living fund). Save away 20% for big-ticket items and travel (fun fund). For the remaining 70%, you can spend it on living expenses. Initially, pay from your checking account for things like utilities and your mortgage. After you've paid the bills, the remaining money is for everyday expenses.

Depending on your personality, you might want a strict monthly budget. If this is you, buy some envelopes for your cash. Each packet will represent a month's budget for a given expense: eating out, clothing, entertainment, etc. Financial advisors highly recommend the envelope system. Figure out how much you want to spend in the categories that could be paid for with cash. Each time you use money, you pull it out of the correct envelope. When a container is empty, you don't get to spend any more in that category until the next month. If you're unhappy with how much money you allocated, make a change for the next month.

If you don't want to be so strict on your budget or you don't have any envelopes, find another method. You could use the simple 70% for living expenses, 20% fun, 10% retirement investment. *But no matter what, you need a budget.* Software and online tools can help track your spending.

The second most important advice your advisor will give you is proper tax planning. If you inherited money in a retirement account, your financial advisor would help prevent unnecessary income tax by setting up an "inherited IRA." Instead of wasting the inheritance on taxes, proper planning can maximize the gift and give 100% of the hard-earned savings to best use.

Advisor, when can I buy the toys?

Let's not forget your toys. You probably have plans in the next couple of years to make all your dreams come true and buy something big. This can (and *should*) happen. It's just a matter of planning for it so you can make your big splurge without jeopardizing your financial well-being. Your financial advisor will help you figure out exactly how much you can spend on your splurges, pulling the money from your fun fund.

To save time, write down your goals before you meet with your advisor. What do you want to have, become, do? What year do you want those? Do you want to run with the bulls in Pamplona, Spain, purchase a sea-plane, buy a beach house? How far away into the future do you want to accomplish your goals? Knowing your aspirations and timeline will be essential to forming a plan. Your goals will dictate when to save and spend. And end up with enough fun fund money for long-term objectives.

Insurance

At your first meeting with your financial advisor, bring with you a list of insurance policies you have as well as information on the amount you pay for them and the forecasted benefit (pay-out). Your financial advisor will help you decide how much life insurance you need. Only consider term life insurance. Other products ("whole life" or "universal life" policies) might sound like they have benefits, but in fact, they aren't worth the costs. A generous term policy that runs for twenty years or so, while your kids are young, will be cost-efficient and (with a payout decided upon by you and your advisor) will fund your kids through college should that sea-plane of yours crash, or the bulls catch up to you in Pamplona.

Get another term policy to safeguard your romantic partner. If you were to die, you want your significant other to continue the same standard of living. You want the second policy because it will need to last longer than the policy for your children. Your advisor will help you calculate a payout amount.

When deciding how much life insurance you need, an advisor will take into account:
- How much money you already have
- Length of time the children might need the money, or your partner might need the money
- Your living expenses
- Any debts you might need to repay
- Cost of higher education or trade school for your children

Your financial advisor will explain how other insurance policies can protect you against lawsuits.

You'll need an "umbrella policy." An umbrella policy covers catastrophic issues; risks your automobile or homeowner's policies don't. For example, let's say you're having a party. Twenty people are on the back deck when it collapses. You've got tons of liability. Lawsuits ensue. Homeowner's insurance will pay some, but it has limits. The umbrella policy takes care of a large portion over and above what your homeowner's insurance will pay.

Most sudden wealth recipients need a financial advisor to help make all of these decisions. Hire a professional who is neither a relative nor a close friend. In other words, hire someone you can fire if he or she doesn't do a good job.

As discussed previously, hire an advisor who works for an hourly rate, rather than someone who takes a commission or a percent of the money you invest. The advisors who earn a commission will have too much self-interest in pushing their financial products. You want your financial advisor to have only *your financial interest* in mind when suggesting investment alternatives, not his or her own.

You'll probably end up paying around $300 an hour. Some advisors will do a flat rate for your situation. To invest a few million, an advisor might charge approximately $3,000. Go to them with a plan you've devised from this material and see if they agree with that plan. See if they can make suggestions (that you agree with) to alter the strategy. The final decision about where to invest your money is yours. Go with what makes sense to you.

Go through NAPFA napfa.org/find-an-advisor to narrow your scope of financial professionals. Find a CFP - Certified Financial Planner or an RIA - Registered Investment Advisor. Have the advisor sign an agreement that reads, "I will work to the fiduciary standard at all times, with your situation."

Your attorney

A young man is walking on the campus of Harvard soon after a night of heavy snow. He's trudging through more than a foot of powdery white flakes trying to get to his morning class. As he reaches halfway to class, the snow is gone. Everything is freshly shoveled, and thick chunks of salt scattered on the pavement. As his walk becomes effortless, he looks up at the sign in front of this building - "Harvard Law School" in large letters. Like caring to remove a hazard, lawyers know how to protect you and your money. Now that you've hired your financial advisor, it's time to lawyer up.

The wealthier you are, the more you can count on lawsuits coming your way. People want your money; they'll go after it through lawsuits—some of them frivolous, some legitimate. In either situation, you need a lawyer. You need someone on your side who can guide you, protect you, and tell you how to handle situations. You have a lot of money to preserve and people counting on you. A lawyer and financial advisor can put your money in the right places (such as trusts), so it's less likely to be taken through a lawsuit.

Your attorney (definitely one with expertise in estate planning and trusts) and your financial advisor can work together to minimize your tax liability both before and – more importantly, in the long run – *after* death. When you do die, you'll want your money to pass on to the people you intended for this money to go to as quickly as possible and with the least tax exposure possible. Trusts can protect your money from creditors, help with taxes, and benefit the recipients by avoiding probate court when you die. Go to AcTEC.org (The American College of Trust and Estate Counsel) to begin your search for an attorney with the qualifications you need. Go to Martindale.com to find reviews of potential lawyers. Finally, to find out if the lawyer you're about to hire has liens, foreclosures, or judgments, check his or her name and corporate identifiers at the county clerk's website.

Your accountant: fiscal superhero

Stacy was 19 when she won the lottery; $4.6 million and more publicity than she wanted. She hired an accountant who protected her money and gave her a story. Stacy's money was wasted. She bought a new trailer home for her mom, a motorcycle for her now ex-boyfriend, and spent the rest on parties. But that was just the story. Almost all of the money was secretly protected. Stacy had two homes, one on the east coast and one outside Beverly Hills. She would travel between her homes on her "salary," depending on which party she wanted to attend. Stacy needed the story to escape the constant requests for money from friends, relatives, and even strangers. Accountants – at least *good* accountants – are fiscal superheroes with powerful tools at their disposal to help you manage your money, while at the same time minimizing taxes. And some will even give you a story to tell.

Look for an accountant who will insist you set up an LLC (Limited Liability Corporation) and then help you buy or rent your house through the LLC to protect your privacy and reduce your tax liability. This accountant will also insist you set up a portion of your money in a trust to protect it from creditors and lawsuits (the accountant will work with your advisor and attorney to set up the trust). This accountant can also tell you how to donate to a "donor-advised fund" to limit your taxes.

To find an accountant, begin your search on AICPA, aicpa.org/forthepublic.html. Then look for "Find a CPA." When interviewing potential accountants, listen for them using the term "red flags." If they're continually warning you about red flags, drop them. They don't know how to avoid tax legally. You need an accountant who will minimize your taxes *legally*, without any risk of going to prison.

Your GateKeeper

After your windfall, long-time friends and family will change how they interact with you. This change brings about feelings of isolation and distrust. Those feelings are often only in the head/mentality of the sudden wealth recipient. The recipient will often isolate him or herself because they feel everyone is out to take part of their money. They distrust even friends because they've encountered people trying to take advantage of them, seeking loans and investments. They withdraw from society in an attempt to protect themselves from the barrage of requests. They often go overboard and lump everyone in the same, greedy category. The wealthy then find it hard to talk with people the way they used to.

To relieve some of the feelings of isolation and distrust, find someone to act as your GateKeeper. This person will be the one who can tell people "NO" to money requests. When people ask for money, you send them to the GateKeeper. Your cousin has a "great" business idea but needs to borrow $20,000. Give him the GateKeeper's contact information. This GateKeeper could be your lawyer, financial advisor, accountant, or a fourth person.

The GateKeeper will have forms for the people to fill out. Those forms will ask them to describe their situation, how much money they need, etc. The GateKeeper can weed through the ones you wouldn't be interested in and send them a letter saying: "No, thank you." The other requests that might be of interest to you will be forwarded to you by the GateKeeper for a final decision. The GateKeeper relieves you of the task of having to say, "No-way" to Cousin Mortimer, who thinks that what Florida needs is a downhill, outdoor snow ski resort.

For your mental health, you need a few friends or relatives you can continue to trust, be friends with, talk to, and know they aren't going to be looking for a handout. You'll know who they are. Keep these people close. And perhaps lay down a firm rule: "I don't talk business – or *do* business – with friends or family."

Tip from someone who dealt with sudden wealth

When I signed my first contract, financial planners came out of the woodwork. They all wanted to "help" me with my money. I chose one who promised me he would invest my money and earn a high return. Over ten years, I paid him $1.5 million in fees and had a slightly above-average rate of return. Since then, I pulled my money away from him and hired an hourly paid advisor. I still earn above-average returns and save all those fees.

Chapter 5 - Where to live

When and where to buy a house

Buying a large home in the first year is a huge mistake often made by sudden wealth recipients. Don't do it. They come with hefty property taxes, hefty homeowners' association dues, expensive insurance. Stay away, at least for the moment, until you have your financial bearings and your plans in order.

As you're considering where you want to live, the questions you have to ask yourself are:
- Will I fit in at the new neighborhood?
- Will my kids be able to get along and play with the other kids in the neighborhood?
- Will my neighbors invite me to their social gatherings?
- Will my obnoxious behaviors and toys be allowed in that neighborhood?
- How will having this house, at this location, benefit my day-to-day living?
- Will living here allow me more time to do the things I enjoy?
- Am I closer to attractions that bring my family happiness?

Beyond fitting in, you have to ask yourself some other questions that will alter the decision to buy vs. rent and where you want to live:
- Where do I want to be ten years from now?
- Will I feel trapped by homeownership and feel I can't move for a better job?
- Will my job location likely change within the next ten years?
- Which school district will be important for my kids?
- How far away should I be from the school where my kids will be involved in sports?
- How would I get my kids home from sporting events?

Buying vs. renting a home

There are advantages and disadvantages to buying and renting a home. Knowing which is best for your family can save you not only stress but also a considerable amount of money. Buying a home is not an excellent investment. Investments aren't supposed to continue to cost you money as upkeep with no significant financial return on that investment. Homes typically go up in value an average of 4% a year, not a high rate of return.

On top of a low return on your investment, buying a home has expenses:
- Repairs
- Real estate commissions
- Community dues
- Insurance
- Interest on a loan

There are some considerable advantages to renting. If you're planning on being in a house for less than five years, rent. You can rent an elegant home and try out the neighborhood. If the market value goes down while you're renting, it doesn't affect you. Real estate commissions don't matter to renters. Repairs are the owner's responsibility. Having something new creates a temporary feeling of happiness. Renting will give you the option of moving and a sense of newness. Instead of having to save up for a new roof or heating system, renters can save up to take trips, and have new and different life experiences. Instead of buying that dream home right away, *plan for it*.

Figure out where you want to be, then rent in the same area. See how you like it. Once you know which location is perfect, you can make the decision to buy—taking your time to find just the right place, at the right price.

There are some reasons you might want to buy a home, or your significant other might feel homeownership is necessary.

Their arguments to owning a home are legitimate and will include:
- The house can build 4% a year in equity
- I can decorate and make improvements
- A sense of stability
- I don't want the neighbors to view me as a temporary (renting) resident
- Predictable and stable costs, unlike rent going up
- A tax deduction on the interest of a mortgage and property taxes paid
- Capital gains aren't taxed

Buying or renting—no single solution is right for everyone. Take stock of your priorities, and then consult with your financial team as to what is the best route for you to take.

Tip from someone who dealt with sudden wealth

Renting opens up options. Those who rent their home can jump at the next opportunity. By renting, you're not building an investment in a property; you're investing in YOU.

Chapter 6 - Psychology behind your windfall

With this money, I'm feeling numbness, fear, with a touch of excitement

An element of trepidation comes packaged with everything new that we encounter, even sudden wealth. After all, being rich is new and unknown terrain for you. And we all have a natural fear of the unknown, no matter how enticing that unique situation might be.

These feelings will pass. You will become adjusted to your new situation, and it will become your new "normal." You will become accustomed to the changes in your lifestyle, habits, and outlook. And in the end, it will be all for good. . . or maybe the pre-money, simple life was better / safer / less stressful.

I'm feeling unworthiness, resentment, guilt, with a touch of revulsion

If you feel any sense of unworthiness, resentment, guilt, or disgust concerning your windfall, you should talk to a professional psychological counselor. Unworthiness, resentment, and guilt are indications you have issues with the way you got this money. If you're feeling aversion, you have a psychological problem with the person who gave you the money. If you have unresolved feelings of avoidance or anger, you are highly likely to spend all your windfall or give it away to alleviate these bad feelings. Perhaps the money came to you from a relative, you and others despised or was a criminal. You feel the inheritance is tainted. Don't let your memory of the person influence your decisions with this money.

Of most importance, while you're in this state of confusion, don't take any drastic steps with your money, such as giving away your windfall. Start with putting your money into an irrevocable trust for three years. Use this time to talk with a psychiatrist or psychologist about your feelings. After three years, if you still feel you want to give it all away or take some other such drastic step, talk to a financial advisor. Find out how to grow the fund and then make yearly donations that can last thirty or more years instead of a quick shotgun blast.

With this money, I've stopped enjoying life

It seems hard to imagine so soon after you got this windfall, but many wealthy people stop enjoying life. If this happens to you in the future, you'll have retreated. You think people treat you differently now or are only interested in your money. Get back to doing the things you enjoy and being with the people who make you happy. Stay away from self-medicating drugs and alcohol.

To enjoy life again, find your passion, find fun, or reinvent yourself. Try racecars or skydiving, or something tame like landscape painting. The point here is to interact with new people. Find new friends who don't necessarily know your background. People who can accept you for who you want to be, not what happened to you.

This money has brought stress

You would think having a ton of money would reduce stress. It does reduce the tension of paying the bills, but it carries on other strains most people don't enjoy. To help this feeling, take a step back. Take a break. Have your financial advisor park your money in safe, stable investments. Live on the small salary your advisor sets up. Take a part-time job to get your mind off the responsibility this money has brought you. Hire people to relieve stress. Let your financial team worry about the money.

I don't want to come across as being spoiled

If you spend money in a way contrary to what most adults would see as responsible, you'll be seen as spoiled. Everyone has different opinions about what is responsible spending.

To keep people from seeing you as spoiled, you have three choices:
- Spend money the way THEY think is appropriate
- Keep your spending a SECRET
- NOT CARE what other people think

Go for the last option. It doesn't matter how you got this sudden wealth. It's your money, and you have a plan in place that will make this money last. You're not spending it frivolously. You're setting goals. You're accomplishing those goals, and you're having a blast doing it. Let those people talk behind your back. You've got one thing they don't have—money. All they have is envy.

I don't want to come across as being selfish

Being generous is one of the greatest acts you can do with this money. Giving to those in genuine need can go a long way for both your mental well-being and the people getting a leg up. On the other hand, be cautious of people hearing of your windfall and acting out of greed. You don't owe them a single thing. No need to explain as to why you don't feel like raining money down on your friends and relatives. Use your canned response: Send them to the GateKeeper.

I inherited a company

Congratulations, you are now the owner of a company someone else was successful at running. Now you have to live up to that standard. Good luck. Consider hiring people to run it for you. You may not have the expertise or the knowledge to run this company. Ask the people in charge of their opinion of you taking an active role. If you choose to take an active part, you'll need to act like a boss.

The boss always speaks last. The boss will ask clarifying questions, but not give their opinions until everyone has shared theirs. Waiting to express your opinion, accomplishes two things. First, it makes people feel valued. Second, it gives you the chance to formulate the best possible solution. If you were to give your opinion in the beginning, yes-people would simply agree with you.

As an owner of a company, hire people who don't think like you. Look for people with opposing points of view, which you may not have considered. Hire people who are well-qualified in your industry. Hire people away from competing companies. Hire people smarter than you. When people contemplate taking a job, they want to know their work will make a difference in the company. As you're interviewing them, let them know you're going to be relying on their opinions, on their knowledge, and their background. People want to feel valued.

If you aren't the type of person to run a business, consider selling it or letting other people run it for you. Before you sell the company, ask yourself if you have a responsibility to the employees. What will happen to them? These people had relationships with your relative, built over the years. Do other options exist to pull money out of the business? Your financial advisor, lawyer, and accountant can help you reach your goals, and getting this team together at once will be one expensive lunch.

You can be the person behind the scene who gets to use the profit for their own living expenses while other people do the work. You don't have to take an active role in this company. You may not be qualified to run this company, but you can hire people who are experts. Hire people you trust, promote those people your relative or benefactor trusted. Find people who want to grow the company, and have a plan to increase profits.

Tip from someone who dealt with sudden wealth

I have to live a secret life. I can't post just any pic on social media. When I do, I get shit from all over. The haters are out there, and they create this negative cloud. I've got to ignore 'em. Live my own life, but still be careful about what I put out there.

Chapter 7 - Your money's impact

Making promises

Stop making promises related to your windfall. You need to make decisions for your money in conjunction with tax, estate, and investment planning to keep the money for the future you. If you've already made some promises, you might have to make good on them. You're a person of your word. You promised to give your brother a few bucks; pay him. You promised to give your parents some money; fork it over. At this point, don't make any more promises. When people ask for money, use your canned response: Send them to the GateKeeper.

A relative or friend has a business idea

If you haven't already encountered people asking you to invest in their business, you will soon. Cousin Mortimer even comes back with a better idea: an *indoor* downhill snow skiing resort in Florida, like the one they have in Dubai.

Don't mix business with family or friendship. Not ever. Seven out of ten small businesses with employees fail within the first ten years. Your relative or friend is no exception. And they are impossible to play "hardball" with when the "going gets tough," and it's time to start suing people. And even if the business succeeds, there will be inevitable disagreements which will lead to strained relations. Count on it.

Keep your relationships and investments separate. The wealthy need friends. They don't need to change friends into business partners. Simply tell them your money is tied up right now. Or better yet ... well, you know by now ... to the GateKeeper go!

Leaving a legacy

Charitable donations will make you feel good and help other people. Find a few charities that have an emotional impact on you. Make regular and significant donations to those charities; give 'til it feels good. Another possibility is setting up scholarships in the area in which you're interested. Jason set up a scholarship for college students interested in his line of work and were attending the college in which he graduated. He helped young people and quickly found himself sitting on the board of directors for the university. He was giving money and time. Jason was leaving a lasting legacy that would last generations.

If you want this money to have long-lasting meaning, don't focus on the amount. The amount isn't important. Raising responsible children who have values, beliefs, and know how to give is imperative. Incorporate your guiding principles and your values into conversations. Tell stories and lessons about how you failed and prevailed, how you lost money on single stock investments and how you did well with index funds. Tell stories about giving and how it helped people.

In preparing your kids and grandkids for this inheritance, you need to educate them.

Focus on three factors:
1 How to safeguard the wealth
2 How to live off the growth
3 How to be generous

Tell them they need twenty-five times their yearly expenses in passive income-producing investments. With this amount of wealth, they too can withdrawal 4% plus inflation every year.

To leave a legacy for the next two generations, set money aside. Set up and max out Roth IRAs for your adult children. Retirement accounts will be money they can live off when they reach 59 ½ years old. Set up educational trusts for your grandchildren.

If you enjoyed or got something out of reading this book

Thank you. You had plenty of choices, but you picked this one. If you got something out of it, please recommend it to friends and on social media. Please leave an honest review at the store or online vendor where you bought this book.

www.ingramcontent.com/pod-product-compliance
Lightning Source LLC
Chambersburg PA
CBHW080955220526
45465CB00008BA/3298